SCRAP HAPPY
Quick-Pieced Scrap Quilts

by Sally Schneider

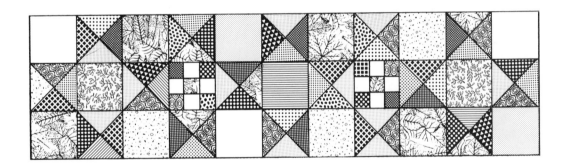

That Patchwork Place ®

CREDITS

Photography . . . . Brent Kane
Illustration and Graphics . . . . . . Stephanie Benson
                                          Nicki Salvin-Wight
Text and Cover Design . . . . Judy Petry
Editor . . . . Liz McGehee

Scrap Happy: Quick-Pieced Scrap Quilts ©
©1990 by Sally Schneider
That Patchwork Place, Inc.,
PO Box 118, Bothell, WA 98041-0118

Printed in the United States of America
97 96 95 94 93   6 5

Library of Congress Cataloging-in-Publication Data

Schneider, Sally.
    Scrap happy : quick-pieced scrap quilts / Sally
Schneider.
       p.   cm.
    ISBN 0-0943574-73-0
    1. Quilting—Patterns. 2. Patchwork—Patterns.
    I. Title.
TT835.S347 1990
746.9'7—dc20
                             90-41389
                                CIP

Contents

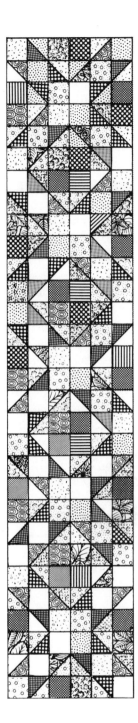

ACKNOWLEDGMENTS

Many people help in the preparation of a book, some without even knowing it. For help on this book, I would like to acknowledge and thank the following people:

Barbara Eikmeier, Manhattan, Kansas, for her persistent encouragement and for quilting Windy City;

Evie Griffin and the staff at the Quilt Barn in Puyallup, Washington (Nancy, Cheri, Eloise, and Pam), for their enthusiastic support and for taking over some of my responsibilities as my deadline approached;

Jan Davis, Seattle, Washington, who made a Confetti quilt top and became a friend;

Students in Colorado and Hawaii who kept asking for more quick-quilting ideas;

Nan Naubert, Tacoma, Washington, for the use of her Four Patch/Ninepatch quilt;

Lois Boulware, Kaneohe, Hawaii, who suggested the quilting design for Wild Goose Chase;

Betty Flannigan, Excelsior, Minnesota, for helping quilt Good Fences Make Good Neighbors;

Sue Smith, Black Diamond, Washington, for quilting the Ohio Star quilt;

My children, David, Andy, and especially Ted, who have learned to love quilts and to tolerate quick-cooked dinners;

And most of all, my husband, Dick, who has encouraged, supported, suggested, loved, tolerated, edited—and washed a lot of dishes, too.

Introduction

In the past, quiltmaking has been thought of as a way to use up bits and pieces of fabrics and to create something from nothing. This philosophy of "using it up" has been passed from generation to generation and is probably still at the root of why people begin to make quilts. Meeting the expectations of our mothers and grandmothers is a basic behavior pattern taught us as very young children.

Quiltmaking has another element to which I have become attuned in my years as a quilter, particularly in the five years I have worked in quilt shops: Quilting is a sensual activity. Have you ever noticed how difficult it is to keep people from handling quilts at shows? Or, take a moment the next time you are in a quilt shop to watch other people. As they come in, they make a beeline for their favorite-color fabrics. They run their eyes over the selections, they fondle the individual fabrics, and they become absorbed in ideas of how to use them. They "fall in love" with some fabrics and take them home to add to their collections. When they use them in quilts, they remember all those feelings.

Is it any wonder, then, that scrap quilts are so appealing? By providing an opportunity to create something useful and beautiful from something that might otherwise sit unused on a shelf or in a drawer, they evoke a feeling of familiarity, comfort, and warmth.

Traditionally, suggestions for using scraps to make quilts have required that the pieces be cut and sewn together individually. Widespread use of quick-piecing techniques in the early 1980s, however, has changed the contents of many quilters' scrap baskets from small odd-shaped bits of fabric to strips, squares made of two or more triangles, and small pieces of yardage left over from other quick-pieced quilts.

This book will show you how to choose patterns and prepare your scrap baskets with these modern techniques in mind. With proper organization of your fabric and forethought in planning its utilization, piecing a scrap quilt need no longer be a laborious undertaking.

The methods used to make these quilts are standard quick-piecing techniques. All the designs are traditional ones or adaptations of traditional patterns that are typically made of just a few fabrics. Making them as scrap quilts is just a matter of planning how to incorporate these leftover pieces.

Fabrics

Sources for Scraps

Fabrics for making scrap quilts may be extra pieces from a Log Cabin quilt, a quarter-yard left from your first sampler, strips from a strip-quilted vest, or bits and pieces that you couldn't throw away because someday they might be useful. They can be the collection of quarter- and half-yards or remnants with which you began your fabric collection. They even can be pieces trimmed from the sides of grids that you made for quick-pieced triangles. Whatever their origin, all fabrics that you want to use in your scrap quilt should be prewashed 100% cotton.

You can also take some time to cut pieces of fabric from your collection. Every time you begin a new quilt or cut fabric for a smaller project, save just one or two strips of the fabric you are working on. Every time you sew a grid of triangles, make a few extra to put aside for the scrap box. You can even purchase small pieces specifically for scrap quilts. How many times have you gone into your local quilt shop and seen three or four pieces that you really liked but didn't buy because you didn't know what you wanted to do with them? By planning to make these quick-pieced scrap quilts, you can buy a small amount of that fabric and know just how it will be used, with no guessing or wondering if you have enough of one particular fabric. None of the quilts requires any great quantity of a particular fabric, except those few that use a common background fabric.

My students frequently comment that they must use up some of their accumulated fabric before they can acquire more. If you go through your collection and cut ³/₄ yard from each piece and prepare it as described in the next section, you can utilize a significant amount of fabric. Admittedly, it has only been relocated, but now it will be in a place and form in which it can be used easily and quickly. This may encourage you to actually make it into a scrap quilt. At least you will have created room to allow new additions to your collection!

Consider also those few fabrics that you really love, that you have put aside for something special, that you take out and look at every few months, that fill your mind with indecision about whether this is "the right project"—the one that is worthy of this special fabric. I personally had several of those pieces. In fifteen years of quilt-making, I never seemed to find quite the right project. Good ideas had to be discarded because there was not quite enough of this all-important wonderful fabric. I even carried swatches of that fabric in my wallet for several years, hoping I would find more of it. The project had to become another bright idea filed for a later time, and, meanwhile, my stash of special fabrics continued to grow! But, finally, I began to put those special fabrics in my scrap quilts, and I enjoy them every time I see them. My mind is also free of fruitless concern about whether or not I will ever find more of my special fabrics.

Organizing Fabric

All the quilts in this book are constructed from fabric pieces in the following sizes:

1¹/₂" strips
2" strips
2¹/₂" strips
2¹/₂" finished squares made with two
    half-square triangles
 3" finished squares made with two half-square triangles

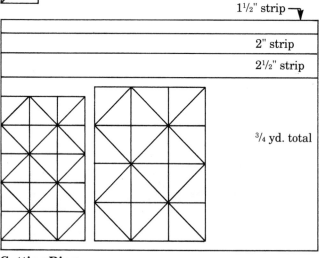

Cutting Diagram

My system of converting fabric into useful scraps is based on cutting a ³/₄ yard length into a 1¹/₂" strip, a 2" strip, and a 2¹/₂" strip. These strips are cut from the full width of the fabric. This leaves slightly more than ¹/₂ yard, which is cut lengthwise into three pieces: The first is 11½" wide, the second is 12½" wide, and the remaining piece will be about 18" square.

The first piece will be paired with another piece of the same size but with a different value (lighter pieces with darker pieces), marked, and sewn with a grid of half-square triangles that finish to 2½" square. The second piece will be paired with another in the same way as the first, then marked and sewn with a grid that finishes to 3" square. The remaining piece can be stored and used later for larger squares or alternating unpieced blocks.

All these pieces should be stored separately from the rest of your fabric collection. I find that clear plastic shoe boxes or sweater boxes from the dime store are perfect for the strips and triangles, using one box for each size of strip and half-square triangle unit. Under-the-bed storage boxes work well for the extra pieces. I fold these pieces and place them in the box like files in a file cabinet, so that I can see everything in the box at a glance. Having small pieces put aside also helps reduce the clutter and work of cutting fabric from the larger yardage in my collection. There aren't large pieces to get out, unfold, iron, cut a small piece from, refold, and put away.

Calculating Yardage

All the quilts in this book were planned for use with the strips and half-square triangles described in the previous section. The individual quilt directions will tell you which size strip or half-square triangle you need for the design. They will also tell you if you need to cut other pieces from your smaller stored pieces. The cutting chart lists the number of strips or half-square triangles to cut. Only when a common background fabric is needed for design purposes is a large amount of yardage specified.

Variety and Value

The National Quilting Association defines scrap quilts for their contest category as those containing at least seventy-five fabrics. In addition, I believe that a good scrap quilt is one whose planning is organized around considerations of value and variety.

Quilters sometimes seem reluctant to make scrap quilts because they are accustomed to coordinating the fabrics for their quilts. The beauty of scrap quilts does not lie in their coordination but, rather, in the abandon with which many fabrics are used together. The smaller the number of fabrics used in a quilt, the more important it is that they complement each other. But, in a scrap quilt, the significance of an individual fabric is greatly diminished. A single piece becomes only a small part of an overall scheme, to which there is only the rhyme and reason of value and design, not fabric coordination.

Varying the scale of the prints can also contribute to successful results. Small flowered prints, larger-scale prints, geometrics, plaids, and stripes cut either lengthwise or crosswise all work well together in scrap quilts. This is a good place to use some of the tropical prints or large-flowered chintzes that are so widely available today. Some of the more unusual fabrics, such as those featuring animals or fish, also give an added dimension to scrap quilts. Solids do not work as well; the intensity of their color tends to make them stand out from the rest of the fabrics, interrupting the flow of the design.

I rarely concern myself with specific colors in a scrap quilt, except for some advice I took from my mother a long time ago. We were discussing flower gardens at the time, but the lesson has been applicable to quilts. She told me that every garden needed some red and some yellow—not too much yellow or it might overpower the rest of the flowers, but just a little scattered throughout. I have tried to follow that advice and have found that it gives my quilts an extra sparkle. They are not as successful without the red and yellow pieces.

When you are making designs with strips, the strips should be separated into light, medium, and dark values, and the required number of strips of a particular value should be chosen for that pattern. Each strip is a different fabric, but because the values remain consistent, the quilts maintain their traditional design. One method for increasing the variety of fabrics in designs pieced with strips is to use just half the length of a strip and double the number of sets required. For example, if a design requires four dark strips and six light strips to be sewn into two sets, you would choose eight half-length dark strips and twelve half-length light strips to make four shorter sets.

In the left group, ten fabrics are arranged by value in order from dark to light. In the middle group, the six darkest fabrics are used; the lightest fabric in this group was a medium in the top group. In the right group, the six lightest fabrics are used; the darkest in this group was a medium in the top group.

If each of the strips is a different fabric, the number of fabrics used in the design is doubled. All the directions for the strip-pieced quilts in this book reflect this idea.

When making designs with half-square triangles, you will want to choose the squares from a stockpile of pieces that use many different fabric combinations. At the same time, however, you will want to maintain the value requirements to retain the integrity of the design.

These are not charm quilts, in which each pattern piece is cut from a different fabric, but rather ones in which a particular fabric is used in several places. A 22" long strip will yield only fourteen 1½" squares, so that a design using those squares will use any one particular fabric only fourteen times. That fabric may always be used in the same combination of strips in a row, but when those rows are scattered throughout a quilt and combined with rows from other sets to make a block, it will not be apparent that it is always used in the same combination.

Variety also encompasses the distribution of fabrics in the quilt. You must be sure that similar fabrics are not all grouped together in the same part of the quilt. If you carefully distribute fabrics throughout the quilt, the result will be more harmonious.

In a group of fabrics placed next to each other, it is not difficult to determine which pieces are darker than the others. Value, then, simply means how dark or light a fabric is in relation to the other fabrics you are using. Pieces should be sorted by their relative value, the darkest ones go in the dark pile, the lighter ones go in the medium pile, and the lightest ones go in the light pile. None of the fabrics in the medium pile should be darker than any in the dark pile, or lighter than any in the light pile.

The value of a particular piece of fabric, then, changes with its companion fabrics. If you choose a range of only light and medium fabrics, a specific piece that was a medium in one group can become a dark in this group if it is darker than the rest of the fabrics. Study the photograph to see how the value of a particular square changes as its companion fabrics change.

Strip Piecing

Many of the designs in this book require strips to be cut a specific width. They can be cut quickly and accurately using specialized tools: a rotary cutter, a cutting mat, and a Plexiglas™ ruler. My favorite ruler is one that is 6" x 24" and has both horizontal and vertical grids marked in ⅛" increments. A few other tools might be useful as well, but these are the essential ones.

To cut with the rotary cutter, push it along the edge of the ruler, using a smooth motion and consistent pressure. Always push the cutter away from you, both for safety reasons and because it is easier to push with your whole body than to pull with just your arm muscles. If the blade does not cut through all layers, press a little harder. With a little experience, you will learn how much pressure to use.

Before cutting strips, you must straighten the edge of your fabric. Begin by folding the ironed fabric in half, matching the selvages.

Selvages

Fold

Fold the fabric again, lining up the fold of the fabric with the selvages. You now have four layers of fabric.

Selvages

Fold

Using your ruler, line up one of its horizontal lines with the folded edge of the fabric (opposite the side with the selvages). Slide the ruler toward the raw edge on the right side of the fabric until it is as close to the edge as possible while still having all four layers of fabric underneath.

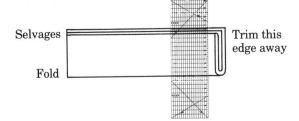

Selvages

Fold

Trim this edge away

Cut along the edge of the ruler, trimming off the uneven edge of fabric. Discard the trimmings. Turn the entire cutting board with the fabric on it so that the trimmed edge is now on your left. When the edges are all straight, use the vertical measuring lines of the ruler to begin cutting strips. Measure the size strips you want by lining up the vertical line that determines your required size with the cut edge of the fabric, and cut.

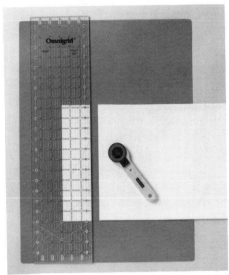

Quick-Pieced Triangles

Half-Square Triangles

To quickly and accurately produce a large quantity of squares consisting of two half-square triangles, use the grid system described in this section. This method requires two pieces of fabric, no larger than 18" x 22" each, placed right sides together, a ruler with a grid marked in $\frac{1}{8}$" increments, and a very sharp pencil or other marking implement. Mechanical pencils and black fine-point ball-point pens work well for marking, as do silver-, white-, or yellow-colored pencils if you keep their points sharp.

Determine the size of the squares for the grid by adding $\frac{7}{8}$" to one of the short sides (finished size) of your half-square triangle. This method requires that you sew a $\frac{1}{4}$" seam allowance on all sides of the triangle, but if your presser foot is not exactly $\frac{1}{4}$", don't despair. (See Making Marking Guides for Grids on page 12.)

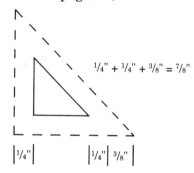

$\frac{1}{4}" + \frac{1}{4}" + \frac{3}{8}" = \frac{7}{8}"$

$\frac{1}{4}"$ $\frac{1}{4}"$ $\frac{3}{8}"$

Place two pieces of fabric right sides together. You can use the pieces described on pages 6–7 or you may use other pieces of fabric. Using either the $\frac{7}{8}$" measurement or your constructed marking guide, begin by drawing a grid of squares on the back of the lightest or easiest-to-mark fabric. Draw a horizontal line on your fabric close to the edge, then measure the required distance from this line and draw another line. Repeat to the end of your fabric.

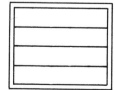

Draw horizontal lines

Line up a horizontal line on your ruler with one of the lines you have drawn to determine an exact 90° angle. With the ruler near the edge of the fabric, draw a vertical line. Measure the required distance from this line and draw another line. Repeat to the end of your fabric. Your fabric will resemble the lines of a checkerboard.

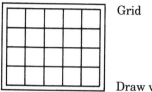

Grid

Draw vertical lines

Now, draw diagonal lines through all the squares. By alternating the direction of the drawn lines, you can arrange the grid so that it can be sewn without ever cutting your thread.

Draw a diagonal line in every other row of squares in one direction,

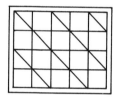

Draw diagonal lines one way

then in every other row of squares in the other direction.

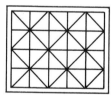

Draw diagonal lines both ways

To check the grid, you should have one diagonal line in each square. If a square has an X through it, it is incorrect and you must redraw your lines.

To help keep the two pieces of fabric from slipping, you can press or pin them before you begin sewing.

By looking at the diagonal lines carefully, you will see that you can trace a continuous line through the whole grid without ever lifting your pencil. Using the same principle, you can also sew a continuous line without ever cutting your thread.

Begin your sewing in a corner. Place the edge of your presser foot on the drawn line and sew in a straight line to the end of the line. With the needle in the down position, rotate the pieces of fabric 90°, then continue sewing to the next corner. Rotate again and sew. Keep rotating 90° and sewing straight lines until you reach the end.

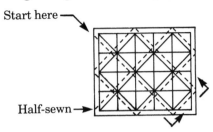

Now, rotate the fabric 180° and sew back to the starting point, being sure to keep the edge of your presser foot on the drawn line. When you are finished, you should have a sewn line on each side of all diagonal lines.

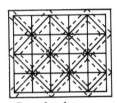

Completely sewn

Cut the grid apart exactly on each drawn line; the result will be two half-square triangle units, already sewn together, for each square of the grid that you drew. The pieces of fabric that you have reserved for these scrap quilts will yield thirty half-square triangle units that finish to $2\frac{1}{2}$" square or twenty-four units that finish to 3" square.

The seams must be pressed to one side or the other; the directions for the specific quilt you are making may tell you which way to press. If not, it is usually safe to press to the darker side.

After you have pressed the seam allowances, you will also find little triangles sticking out beyond the square on two corners. These should be trimmed off to help reduce bulk.

Quarter-Square Triangles

The method for producing quick-pieced half-square triangles can also be used to construct quarter-square triangles by simply changing the size of the grid. For all of the designs in this book, the grid should be $1\frac{1}{4}$" larger than the desired finished size of the square. If your presser foot is not exactly $\frac{1}{4}$" wide, see the section on Making Marking Guides for Grids on page 12.

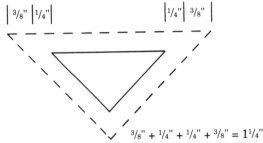

$\frac{3}{8}" + \frac{1}{4}" + \frac{1}{4}" + \frac{3}{8}" = 1\frac{1}{4}"$

Using two half-square triangle units with either identical or different fabrics, place them right sides together, match up seam lines, and draw a diagonal line through the square, crossing the seam line. With the edge of the presser foot on the line as a guide, sew on each side of the diagonal line. Cut on the drawn line and you will have the quarter-square triangle units shown below.

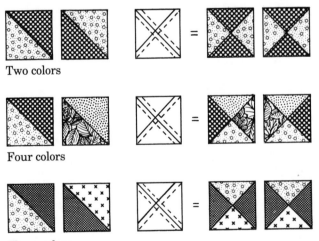

Two colors

Four colors

Three colors

Making Marking Guides for Grids

If your presser foot is not exactly ¼" wide, you must make corrections for this variation when you measure grids for quick-pieced triangles. You can either purchase a foot that is exactly ¼" wide, if one is available for your machine, or you can make your own marking guide that takes this difference into account. To make a guide, you will need heavy template plastic or heavy posterboard. This guide will only be used to draw the checkerboard of squares and will not be used to draw diagonal lines or to cut.

Begin by drawing a square of the required finished size on a sheet of paper. Do not use graph paper. Use the ruler you normally use to cut strips. Be sure the square is as precise as you can possibly make it.

Draw a square

Draw a diagonal line through the square. Extend the line for about 1" at each end.

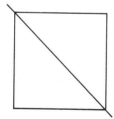

Draw a diagonal line

Remove the thread from your sewing machine and place the right edge of the presser foot on this diagonal line. Stitch a line parallel to the drawn line on the paper.

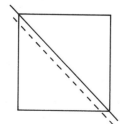

Sew on one side of the line

With your ruler, add ¼" seam allowances to the two adjacent sides of the square opposite the sewn diagonal line. Extend these seam allowances to the sewn line.

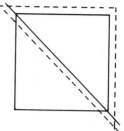

Add ¼" seam allowances

Measure from the top of the square to the intersection of the sewn line and the ¼" seam allowance line. This is the size you want to make your marking guide for making half-square triangles of this particular size.

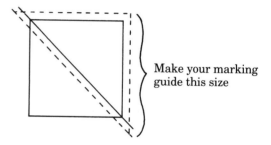

Make your marking guide this size

You will need a different marking guide for each size of half-square triangle you want to make.

This method will also work for quarter-square triangles. Draw a square of the required finished size as you did for half-square triangles, but this time, draw diagonal lines in both directions through the square. Add the ¼" seam allowance to one side of the square.

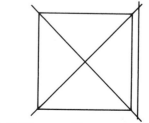

Add ¼" seam allowance to one side

Sewing

With the edge of the presser foot on the diagonal line, sew parallel to both diagonal lines and measure the distance between the intersections of the sewn lines and the ¼" seam allowance line.

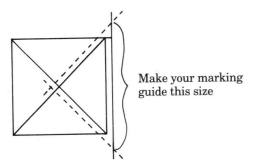

Make your marking guide this size

This is the size of your marking guide.

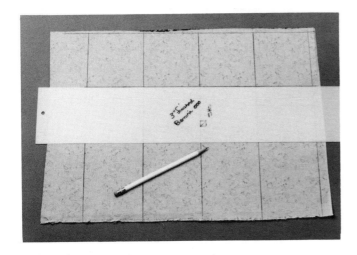

All seam allowances are ¼". Unfortunately, not all presser feet measure ¼", nor are all ¼" measurements on rulers the same. This can lead to inaccuracies in sewing. The solution to this problem is twofold. First, you must be sure that your ruler is accurate and you must always use the same ruler. Some rulers are not printed straight. Check that the ¼" is the same on both sides and both ends of the ruler. Second, using the same ruler again, measure ¼" to the right of your sewing machine needle. Mark it on your machine and follow this mark when sewing. You can use masking tape, a seam guide attachment, if one is available for your machine, or a line drawn with a permanent marker. (This is what I have done.) Test this ¼" seam allowance on a piece of fabric to be sure that you are really sewing ¼".

Sew strips together in the order required for your design (this is called a set). Pressing should be done with a hot iron, without steam. Press the set straight from the right side. Although sets may tend to form a curve, they must be pressed straight. When you have pressed the right side, turn the set over and press from the wrong side, being sure that all seam allowances are pressed flat and to one side. Some directions will specify to which side the seams should be pressed; otherwise, it is usually safe to press the seams toward the darker fabric.

Now, you are ready to cut across these sets at specified intervals to form rows or blocks for your quilt. Using the seam lines as horizontal guides for your ruler, straighten the edge of the set.

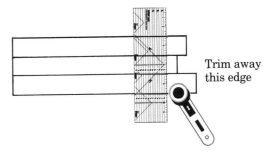

Trim away this edge

The selvage of the fabric is removed in this step. You can usually cut two or three sets of strips at one time; any more tend to slip out of position and become inaccurate.

To sew rows together, match the intersecting seam lines, having seam allowances lie in opposite directions. Pin intersections on either side of the actual seam through the seam allowances.

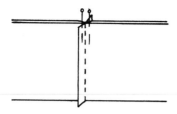

When matching points of triangles, keep the point you must match on top so that you can see it. You will be able to see an intersection of seams on the wrong side of the squares. It looks like a Y.

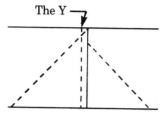

Be sure to sew right through the intersection of the seams so that the point is not cut off.

If you must match a point to a point, as in eight-point centers, push a pin directly through both points and pull it snug. Place a second pin to either side of the first pin, through the seam allowances, and remove the first pin. Stitch through the intersection of the seams.

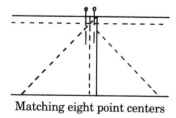

Matching eight point centers

Press seams as you sew them, being careful not to stretch or otherwise distort bias edges.

Diagonal Sets

Setting the blocks of a quilt on the diagonal (on point) rather than straight is a technique that can make many designs more interesting. Some patterns look much better when set on the diagonal, and some patterns are pieced more easily if they are planned as diagonal sets. The piecing of these quilts is no more difficult than of quilts set straight, but there are some tricks for making it easier to handle them.

When blocks are set on the diagonal, there are triangular shapes on the edges and corners that must be filled, either with partial pieced blocks or with plain triangles. I usually fill them with plain triangles, because they are so much easier to construct.

Edge triangles must be cut with the straight grain of the fabric on the longest edge of the triangle. This allows the outside edge of the quilt to be on the straight rather than the bias grain of the fabric, making it easier to attach the borders without stretching the quilt top. To make edge triangles:

1. Measure the diagonal of your completed block.

2. Add 2" to that measurement. Use this new measurement to cut squares of your chosen fabric.

3. Cut the squares in quarters diagonally.

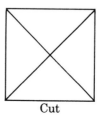
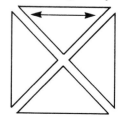

Cut

These triangles are much larger than necessary for your quilt, but because sewing places stress on bias edges, the outside edges tend to curve inward. Therefore, if you cut the triangles with only the standard seam allowance, they would shrink inward during stitching and might end up being too small. It is so easy to trim off the edge and impossible to add more to it!

Place these triangles in the spaces at the edge of your quilt and piece them in as you sew the rows together, following the diagram.

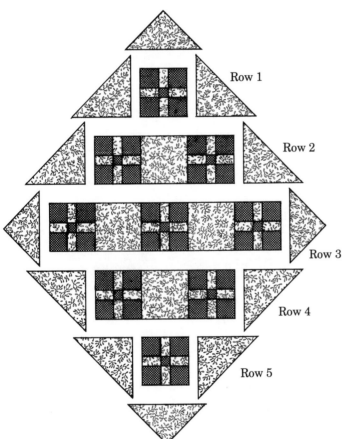

Notice that the right angles of the triangles are lined up with the edges of the blocks, and the other points of the triangles are allowed to overhang the blocks. It is very important to keep that edge straight. When you are sewing one row to another, you can easily stitch over the points that stick up and trim them off after the row has been sewn.

Corners are cut from squares that are the same size as your pieced squares. These squares are cut in half on the diagonal to yield two triangles. You will need to cut two of these squares for every quilt you make and set on the diagonal.

Corner triangles

Before attaching borders to your quilt, you will need to trim the sides and square up the corners. Fold the quilt top carefully into quarters, matching all four corner blocks. Pin through the corners of all four blocks.

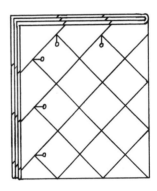

Line up and pin the corners of all the blocks on the edges of your quilt in the same way. With a large acrylic square or another similar right-angled tool, measure 1/4" seam allowance out from the corners of the blocks. Mark and cut along the edges of the blocks.

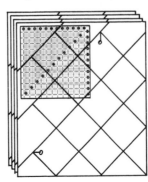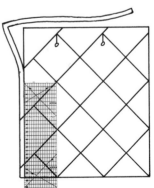

Borders

Borders that are longer than the width of the fabric may be pieced. Cut strips as required and join them with a ¼" seam. You may want to cut a strip in half and add one of the halves to each of two border strips to achieve the necessary length. Measure the border strips for the quilt after you have joined the pieces together. The center dimension and the outside edges of a quilt must be the same measurement in order for a quilt to hang or lie straight. The length of border pieces is determined by measuring the quilt through the center and trimming the border strips to exactly that length.

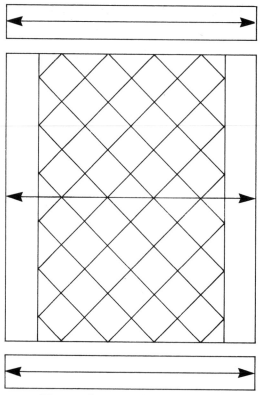

Measure for top and bottom borders

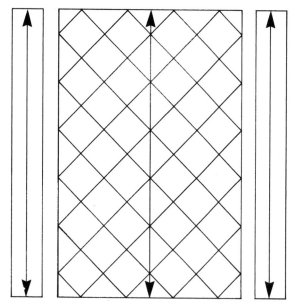

Measure for side borders

When you have cut the strips for the border, fold them in half, then in quarters, and mark the divisions with a pin. Do the same with the quilt, marking the half and quarter points of each side. Matching your markings and easing if necessary, pin the seam every few inches; stitch. Repeat the steps for each border you put on, and you will have a nice, flat, straight quilt when you are finished.

Before your quilt is basted, use care when handling it, particularly if it is a diagonally set quilt. The vertical and horizontal lines of these quilts are on the bias and will stretch easily. While basting, it is important to pat the quilt flat, rather than try to push fullness to one edge or the other. You must also be careful that you do not stretch or distort the fold lines when you fold up the unquilted and unbasted top. You may stretch the center of the quilt to the point where it will never lie flat again!

Gallery of Quilts

Log Cabin Twice Removed *by Sally Schneider, 1987,*
Honolulu, Hawaii, 44" x 58". Red and yellow small squares highlight the dark and
light scrap strips of this Log Cabin variation.

Primitive Pieced Hearts *by Sally Schneider, 1988, Puyallup, Washington, 35" x 45". This quilt features a bright white background that contrasts with the pieced hearts. Alternating plain squares allow plenty of space for hand or machine quilting.*

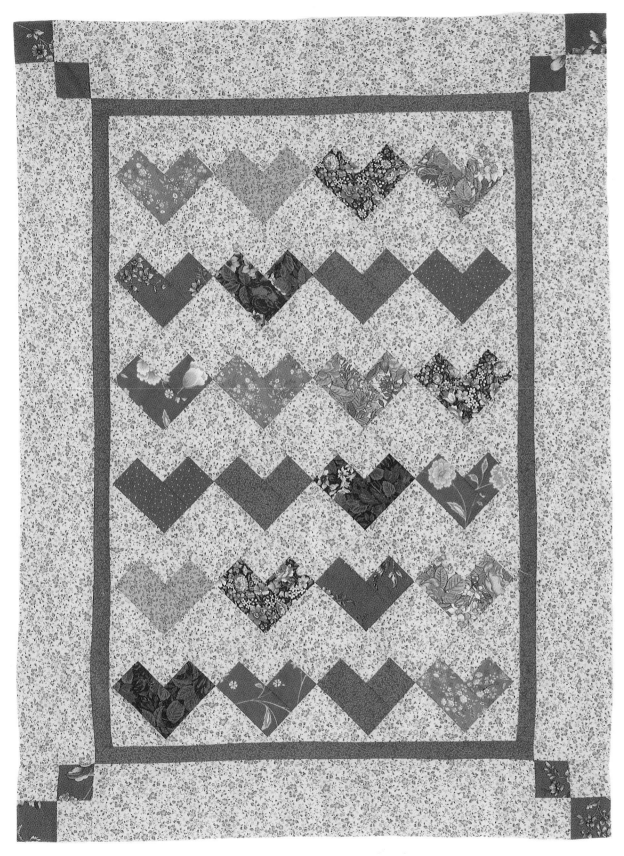

Primitive Pieced Hearts *by Sally Schneider, 1990, Puyallup, Washington, 33" x 44". A print background and easy-to-piece Four-Patch corners soften the look of the hearts.*

Four Patch/Ninepatch *by Sally Schneider, 1987, Honolulu, Hawaii, 62" x 76".*
Using just two color families and a solid-color background produces an argyle effect, with
intersecting squares on the diagonal.

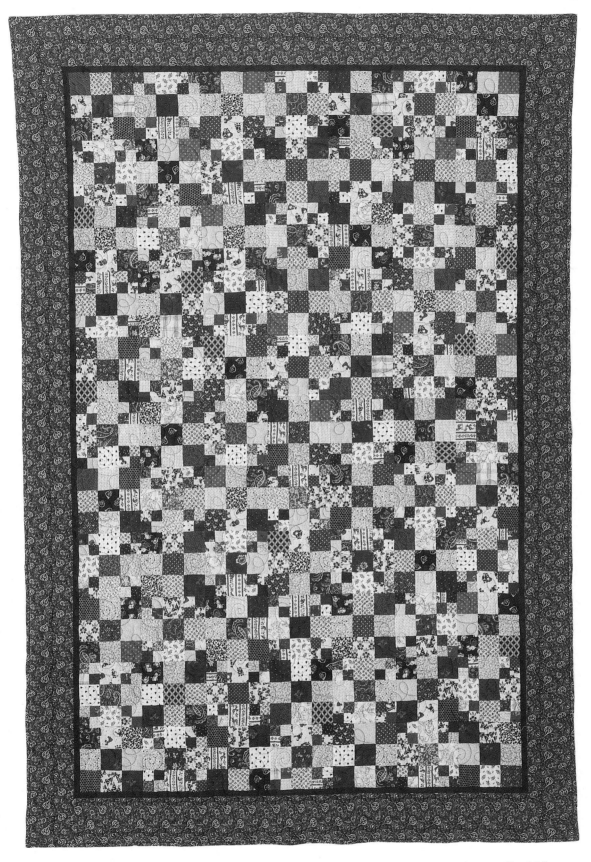

Four Patch/Ninepatch *by Nan Naubert, 1989, Tacoma, Washington, 64" x 92".*
The multitude of red and green prints and the print background make this quilt sing of
Christmas. Machine quilted by J & B Enterprises.

Windy City *by Sally Schneider, 1989, Puyallup, Washington, 37" x 43". A simple design in a diagonal set, this quilt uses some favorite fabrics. Quilted by Barbara Eikmeier.*

Scrap Ninepatch *by Sally Schneider, 1989, Puyallup, Washington, 66" x 82". Using both dark and light values for alternating plain squares gives this quilt the illusion of borders.*

Double Irish Chain by Sally Schneider, 1989, Puyallup, Washington, 62" x 77". Use of a common background fabric retains the traditional design elements while utilizing scraps.

Cinderella *by Sally Schneider, 1988, Puyallup, Washington, 65" x 86". Two simple pieced blocks and plain squares alternate to form stars within stars.*

Good Fences Make Good Neighbors *by Sally Schneider, 1988, Honolulu, Hawaii, 78" x 90". Rail Fence strips separate a bevy of colorful pinwheels. Quilted by Sally Schneider and Betty Flannigan.*

Split Ninepatch *by Sally Schneider, 1989, Puyallup, Washington, 46" x 63"*
Scrap triangles and plain squares make wonderful stars, and the many different fabrics give the quilt a movement of its own.

Wild Goose Chase by Sally Schneider, 1989, Puyallup, Washington, 35" x 35".
A diagonal set makes this quilt easy to piece, and the consistent coloration of the Pinwheel and
"Broken Dishes" blocks adds continuity.

Confetti *by Jan Davis, 1989, Kirkland, Washington, 49" x 59". Primary colors and a common background fabric make a bright baby quilt.*

Confetti *by Sally Schneider, 1989, Puyallup, Washington, 39" x 39". Dark and light scraps and the combination of two blocks produce both small and large pinwheels spinning across the surface.*

Fireworks by Sally Schneider, 1990, Puyallup, Washington, 60" x 82". The use of bright sparks in this basically dark quilt gives it an exciting luminescence.

Ohio Star *by Sally Schneider, 1989, Puyallup, Washington, 45" x 56". A traditional block takes on a new feeling when made with scraps. The alternating plain squares allow you to highlight your special favorites. Quilted by Sue Smith.*

Quilt Plans

The dimensions given in the quilt pattern directions refer to the cut size of the fabric. The $\frac{1}{4}$" seam allowance is included in the dimensions. Do not add seam allowances.

All the quilts in this book use the strips and quick-pieced triangles described previously. The Cutting Chart will tell you which size strip or quick-pieced triangle you need for each design. It will also tell you if you need to cut elements from your extra pieces. The fabric requirements list the number of strips or half-square triangle units used. Only when a common background fabric is preferred for design purposes is a yardage amount specified, as in Primitive Pieced Hearts, Four Patch/Ninepatch, Double Irish Chain, and Confetti.

Strips listed in the Cutting Chart are cut across the full width of the fabric, then cut in half so that they are 22" long. Sets of strips sewn together with half-length strips are also 22" long.

When sewing grids of quick-pieced triangles from the pieces of fabric that are earmarked for this purpose, draw the grid on the lighter pieces of fabric. Each section will yield either twelve or fifteen squares, depending on the size of the grid. Before you sew the grid, you can cut it into two sections and pair each section with a different dark fabric, which will allow further variety in your quilts. These cut sections may contain unequal numbers of squares, such as six squares in one section and nine squares in the other. One drawn square will yield two half-square triangles, so a grid of six squares will yield twelve half-square triangles and a grid of nine squares will yield eighteen half-square triangles.

Please refer to pages 14–16 for general instructions on cutting edge and corner triangles and adding borders. All borders in this book are cut on the crosswise grain of the fabric and pieced where necessary. If you prefer to cut your borders lengthwise, you will need to purchase additional fabric.

Amounts of fabric needed for backings and bindings can be found in the Quilt Finishing chapter on pages 69–70.

Grid of 6 squares

Grid of 9 squares

Primitive Pieced Hearts
Color photos on pages 18 and 19

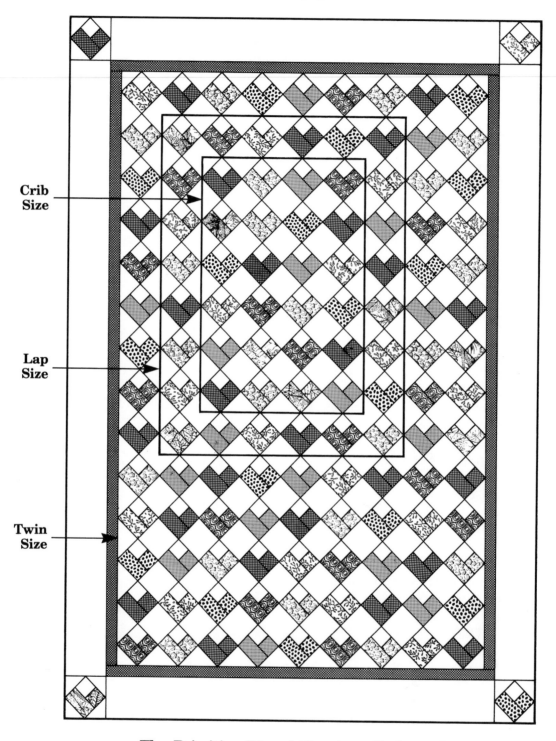

Crib Size

Lap Size

Twin Size

The Primitive Pieced Hearts quilt is made from 2½" strips that are simply pieced into Four-Patch blocks. Using a diagonal set and background fabric for one of the block corners creates the pattern of hearts. You may use one fabric or many different fabrics for the hearts

Cutting Chart

Block size (finished): 4"			
Quilt size	Crib	Lap	Twin
without borders	22" x 34"	34" x 45"	49" x 77"
with borders	35" x 47"	47" x 58"	62" x 90"
Heart blocks	28	52	130
Background blocks	15	35	104
Heart fabric			
2½" strips	10	18	44
Hearts*	28	52	130
Background fabric	1⅝ yds.	2⅜ yds.	4½ yds.
2½" strips	2	4	9
4½" strips	2	4	12
4½" squares**	15	35	104
8½" squares for edge triangles	4	6	11
4½" squares for corners	2	2	2
Outside border (background)			
6¼" strips	4	5	7
Inside border (dark)	¼ yd.	⅓ yd.	⅜ yd.
1½" strips	4	5	7

*One 22" strip of fabric will make three hearts.
**If making heart blocks for border corners, cut 8 more of these squares for each size.

PIECING

1. Cut 8" from each of the strips of heart fabric. Reserve the remainder for a later step.
2. With right sides together, sew the 8" pieces of heart fabric one after the other to each of the 2½" background strips.
3. Press seams toward the darker fabric.
4. Cut each group apart at 2½" intervals. You should have three rows from each heart fabric.

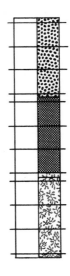

5. Sew each row to the reserved strip of matching heart fabric and trim it even with the two-patch segment. Press toward the dark fabric.

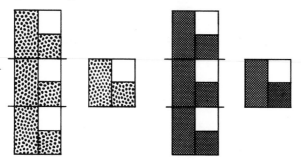

6. Arrange the heart and background blocks; use the edge and corner triangles to fill in the edges and corners (see Diagonal Sets on page 14).

7. Trim corners and edges of quilt as described on page 15.

BORDERS

1. To construct heart blocks for the border corners, take eight 4½" squares of background fabric and cut each square into two triangles. (You will now have sixteen triangles.) Sew one triangle to each side of all four heart blocks.

Heart blocks for corners

2. Attach borders as described on page 16. The inside border uses a dark fabric; the outside border uses the background fabric.

3. Trim the heart blocks for the corners, if necessary, and sew them to each end of the top and bottom border strips.

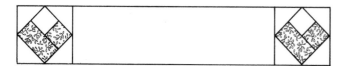

Sew heart blocks to top and bottom border pieces

Creative Option: If you prefer, you may use Four-Patch blocks made in the same way as the heart blocks for the corners of the quilt. These are easier to construct from 2½" strips. You will need to cut the outside border strips 4½"instead of 6½", so the quilt will be slightly smaller.

Four Patch/Ninepatch

Color photos on pages 20 and 21

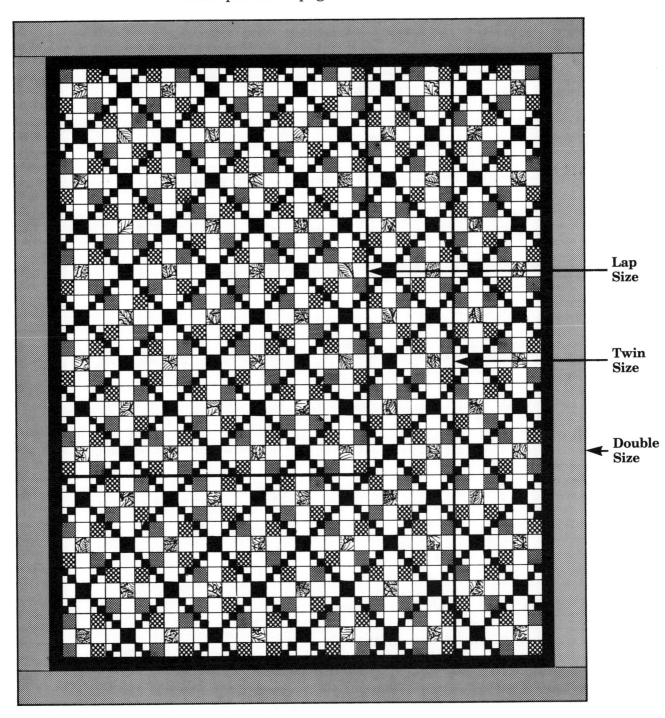

Lap
Size

Twin
Size

Double
Size

Derived from the traditional Double Nine-patch pattern, the Four-Patch/Ninepatch design has an old-fashioned look. Ninepatch blocks with Four-Patch corners are paired with alternating Ninepatch blocks, forming intersecting diagonal lines and creating a great deal of movement. It is a particularly good design for using pieces in just two color families.

Cutting Chart

Block size (finished): 6"			
Quilt size	Lap	Twin	Double
without borders	42" x 54"	54" x 78"	66" x 78"
with borders	52" x 64"	64" x 88"	76" x 88"
Ninepatch blocks with			
Four-Patch corners	31	58	71
Ninepatch blocks	32	59	72
Dark fabric			
1½" strips	19	34	41
2½" strips	24	48	54
Light fabric*	1⅝ yds.	3⅛ yds.	3½ yds.
1½" strips	19	34	41
2½" strips	32	64	72
2½" squares	64	116	142
Inside border	¼ yd.	⅜ yd.	½ yd.
1½" strips	5	6	8
Outside border	⅞ yd.	1 yd.	1⅛ yds.
4½" strips	6	7	8

*If all lights are cut from just one fabric, you will need yardage as indicated and you will need to cut just half the number of light strips.

PIECING

There are two different blocks in this pattern: a Ninepatch block with Four-Patch corners and a simple Ninepatch block.

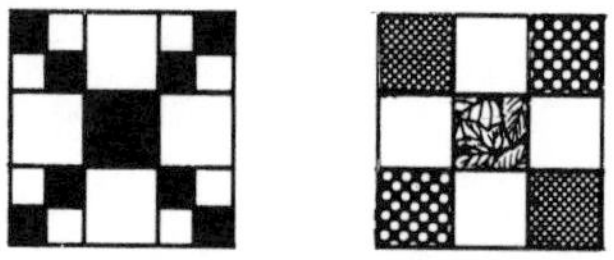

Four Patch   Ninepatch

Ninepatch Blocks with Four-Patch Units

1. Referring to the Cutting Chart, sew the 1½" light and dark strips together in pairs; then, cut them apart at 1½" intervals. Sew the rows together in sets of two to make Four-Patch units:

Lap 124   Twin 232   Double 284

2. Sew a Four-Patch unit to each side of a 2½" light square for Rows 1 and 3. Check position of the dark squares of the Four-Patch unit.

3. Using 2½" strips of light and dark, sew together sets for Row 2:

Lap 4   Twin 8   Double 9

Cut apart at 2½" intervals.

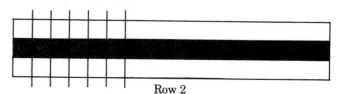

Row 2

4. Rechecking the position of the dark squares in the Four-Patch units, assemble blocks:

Lap 31   Twin 58   Double 71

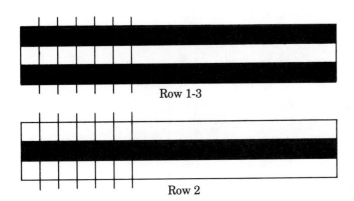

Ninepatch Blocks

1. Sew sets of strips together as shown below.

	Rows 1-3	Row 2
Lap	8	4
Twin	15	8
Double	18	9

Row 1-3

Row 2

2. Cut apart at 2½" intervals. Sew rows together into blocks as shown below.

Lap 32   Twin 59   Double 72

Assembly

1. Arrange blocks according to the quilt plan found on page 37. Alternate Ninepatch with Four-Patch corners and Ninepatch blocks, putting a Ninepatch block in each corner. Sew these blocks together as follows:

Crib	7 x 9
Twin	9 x 13
Double	11 x 13

2. Sew blocks together in rows; then, sew rows together, matching seams where necessary.

Borders

Making inside border first, sew strips together as necessary to provide needed length. Measure, pin, and sew strips to the longest sides

Log Cabin Twice Removed
Color photo on page 17

Crib Size

This design was adapted from a Log Cabin variation called Alabama. When the blocks are put together, there are double small squares of the same color where the blocks meet. But when one strip is removed from the center of the whole design both vertically and horizontally, the design flows much better and justifies the name "Log Cabin Twice Removed." The sewing is more complicated, but the results are worth the extra effort.

All strips are cut 1½" wide. For this particular quilt, you can use the full width of the fabric rather than a half width. Some strips in the following directions are identified by color for clarity only; substitute the color of your choice.

Cutting Chart

Block size (finished): 9"				
Quilt size	Crib	Lap	Twin	Queen
without borders	36" x 54"	54" x 72"	72" x 90"	90" x 90"
with borders	46" x 64"	64" x 82"	82" x 100"	100" x 100"
Log Cabin blocks	24	48	80	100
Light strips	26	52	86	108
Dark strips	26	52	86	108
Yellow fabric	³/₈ yd.	³/₄ yd.	1¹/₈ yds.	1³/₈ yds.
1¹/₂" strips	8	15	24	30
Red fabric	¹/₂ yd.	⁷/₈ yd.	1¹/₄ yds.	1³/₄ yds.
1¹/₂" strips	9	17	27	34
Inside border	¹/₄ yd	³/₈ yd.	¹/₂ yd.	⁵/₈ yd.
1¹/₂" strips	5	7	8	9
Outside border	³/₄ yd.	1 yd.	1¹/₄ yds.	1¹/₂ yds.
4¹/₂" strips	5	7	9	9

PIECING

1. To make the Ninepatch center blocks, sew sets as shown below:

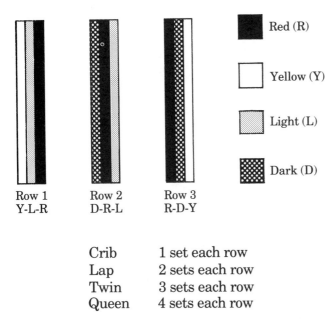

Row 1
Y-L-R

Row 2
D-R-L

Row 3
R-D-Y

Red (R)

Yellow (Y)

Light (L)

Dark (D)

Crib	1 set each row
Lap	2 sets each row
Twin	3 sets each row
Queen	4 sets each row

Cut sets apart at 1¹/₂" intervals. Assemble the Ninepatch blocks.

Crib 24   Lap 48   Twin 80   Queen 100

2. Cut the remaining red and yellow strips into 1¹/₂" squares.

3. Sew a red square to one end of each of your light and dark strips; sew a yellow square to the other end of each strip.

4. Following the diagram below, hold the Ninepatch block right side up with the light sides on the right and on the bottom. Choose a light strip from your pile and fold the yellow square back so that the seam allowance is exposed. With right sides together, match the raw edge of the yellow square of the Ninepatch block with the raw edge of the strip. Begin sewing somewhere in the middle of the yellow square of the Ninepatch block. The yellow square from the strip will extend beyond the block and will be sewn later. Sew to the end of the block and cut the light strip even with the end of the block.

Sew

Cut

Turn the light strip around so that you are holding the end with the red square. Match the seams of the red squares. Sew the entire seam and cut the strip even with the end of the block.

5. With a dark strip from your pile, match seams of yellow squares and sew to the end of the block. Cut the strip even with the end of the block.

Turn the strip around, match red seams, and sew.

Sew to here

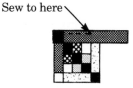

When you get to the end of this row, cut the strip even with the end of the block. Fold up the yellow square left hanging from the first step and complete the seam.

Complete seam

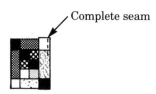

You have completed one round. Repeat for two more rounds, alternating light and dark as above. Make blocks as follows:

Crib 15   Lap 35   Twin 63   Queen 81

6. To make the blocks with the strip "removed," follow diagrams.

Block A
Make one each size

Block B
Crib   2
Lap   3
Twin   4
Double 5

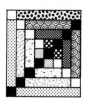

Block C
Crib   1
Lap   2
Twin   3
Double 4

Block D
Crib   2
Lap   3
Twin   4
Double 4

Block E
Crib   3
Lap   4
Twin   5
Double 5

Block F
Crib   15
Lap   35
Twin   63
Double 81

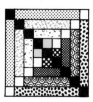

7. When blocks are completed, arrange them according to the diagram on page 40 for crib size. For lap, twin, and queen sizes, see diagram on page 71. Sew blocks together.

BORDERS

Add borders, if desired. The quilt pictured on page 17 has two borders: a light narrow border on the inside and a dark wide border on the outside.

Windy City
Color photo on page 22

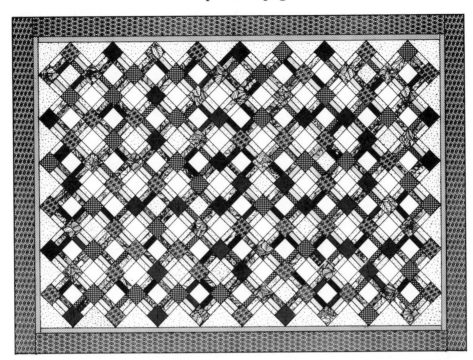

Twin Size

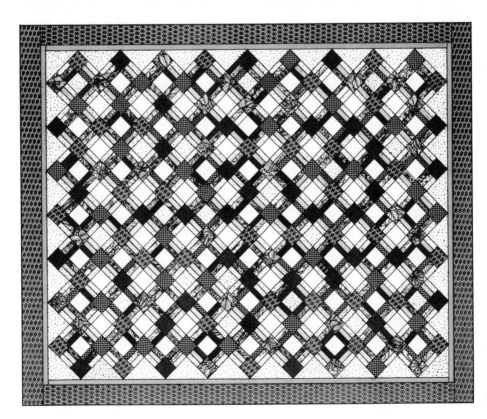

Double Size

This design was pictured in *Country Living* magazine in May 1984 as a simple Amish quilt thrown over the back of a sofa. When the pattern is broken down into its simplest parts and set on the diagonal, it becomes a dynamic design particularly suitable for scraps. Short sets of strips (22″) are used, giving you the opportunity to use a large number of different fabrics.

Crib Size

Cutting Chart			
Block size (finished): 3"			
Quilt size	Crib	Twin	Double
without borders	30" x 39"	55" x 81"	64" x 81"
with borders	40" x 49"	65" x 91"	74" x 91"
Rail fence units	48	216	252
Sets for rail fence	8	36	42
1½" light strips	8	36	42
1½" medium strips	8	36	42
1½" dark strips	8	36	42
3½" squares			
Dark	31	123	142
Light	18	74	111
Edge and corner triangles	⅝ yd.	1 yd.	1 yd.
11" squares for edge			
triangles (10 triangles)	3	7	7
10" squares for corner			
triangles (4 triangles)	2	2	2
Inside border	¼ yd.	⅜ yd.	⅜ yd.
1½" strips	4	7	7
Outside border	⅝ yd.	1 yd.	1 yd.
4½" strips	4	7	8

PIECING

1. Sew strips together in sets using light, medium, and dark, in that order.

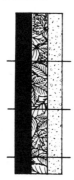

2. Cut the sets into 3½" squares.
3. Arrange the pieced and plain 3½" squares as shown in the diagram on page 43. Sew squares together in rows, then sew rows together in pairs. Sew edge triangles to each end of the pairs of rows. There will be several rows of unequal length, where it may be necessary to sew only part of a seam in order to attach the edge triangles (see the diagram on page 45). Finish sewing the seam after the triangle has been attached. Attach the corner triangles at the very end.

BORDERS

1. Referring to the Cutting Chart, cut 1½" strips and sew them together to achieve the necessary length for your quilt. Measure, pin, and sew as described in the Borders section on page 16.
2. Using 4½" strips for the outside border, sew them together to achieve the necessary length for your quilt. Measure, pin, and sew them to the inside border.

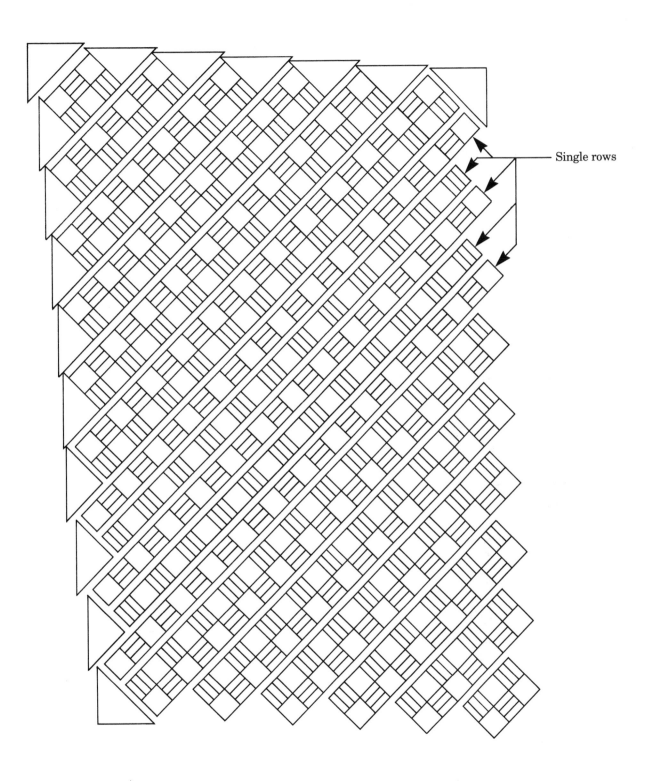

Single rows

Scrap Ninepatch
Color photo on page 23

Setting traditional Ninepatch blocks on the diagonal gives a visually pleasing effect to the design. Varying the darks and lights in the blocks adds a whole new dimension to the quilt. To further vary the darks and lights in the alternating plain squares makes a design that is hardly recognizable as the traditional Ninepatch. Made with scraps, it becomes a real beauty. It is a good idea to include a few light-medium values with your light squares; these add depth to the quilt. Two sizes are given here: lap and twin size. The size changes are achieved by changing the size of the strips and squares, rather than by changing the number of blocks. The strips are cut 22" long.

Cutting Chart		
Block size (finished): 6"		
Quilt size	Lap	Twin
without borders	50" x 62"	66" x 90"
2" strips		
Dark	32	
Medium	11	
Light	35	
2½" strips		
Dark		37
Medium		12
Light		41
5" background		
Dark	5	
Light	58	
6½" background		
Dark		5
Light		58
Edge and corner triangles (dark)		
8½" squares for edge triangles	8	
5" squares for corner triangles	2	
11" squares for edge triangles		8
6½" squares for corner triangles		2

PIECING

1. The values in the Ninepatch blocks in this quilt are arranged in three different ways:

   Make 4   Make 20   Make 56

2. All the blocks are made with just four different sets:

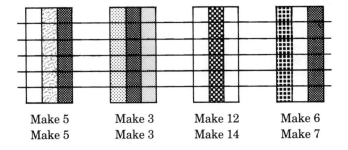

   Make 5   Make 3   Make 12   Make 6   Lap Size
   Make 5   Make 3   Make 14   Make 7   Twin Size

3. Sew strips together. Press all seams toward the darkest fabric.
4. Cut the sets apart at 2" intervals for the lap and at 2½" intervals for the twin.
5. Construct the Ninepatch blocks as shown at left.
6. For edge triangles, you can use eight different squares, all the same dark, or just three or four different darks. Cut them in quarters diagonally.
7. For the corners, cut the squares in half diagonally.
8. Arrange the blocks as shown on page 46. Add edge and corner triangles (see pages 14–15).
9. Sew the blocks together into rows; sew the rows together.

48

Double Irish Chain
Color photo on page 24

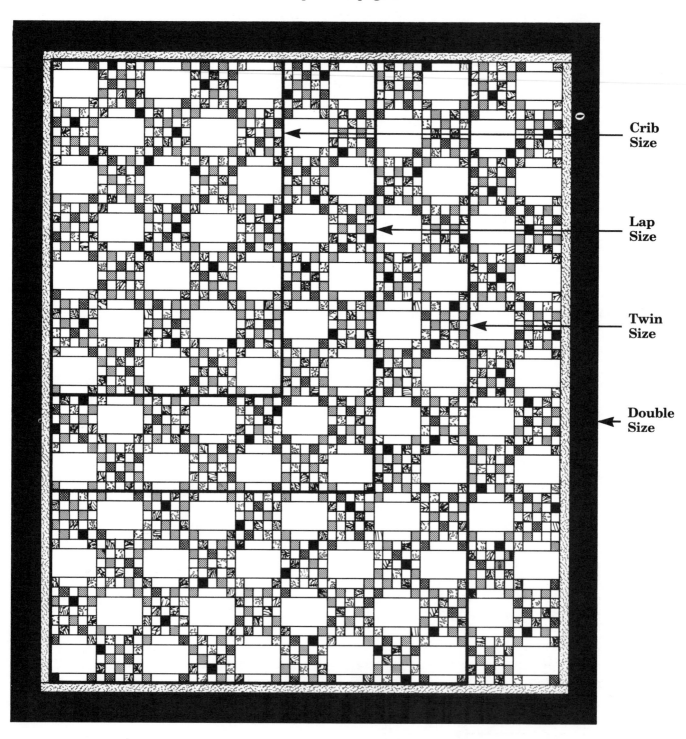

Crib Size

Lap Size

Twin Size

Double Size

The Double Irish Chain pattern is a traditional favorite. It is made with two alternating blocks, both of which are pieced with strips. To adapt the design for scraps, it is best to use one common fabric, either light or dark, for the background. To maintain the integrity of the design, the chains are then constructed of various strips in a value opposite the background.

Cutting Chart					
Block size (finished): 7½"					
Quilt size	Crib	Lap	Twin	Double	Queen
without borders	38" x 53"	53" x 68"	68" x 98"	86" x 98"	
with borders	48" x 63"	63" x 78"	78" x 108"	93" x 108"	95" x 110"
Block 1	**17**	**31**	**58**	**71**	**71**
Block 2	18	32	59	72	72
Scrap fabric					
2" strips	**32**	**55**	**96**	**119**	**119**
Background	2¼ yds.	3 yds.	5¾ yds.	6½ yds.	6½ yds.
2" strips	13	22	39	51	51
5" strips	8	11	18	23	23
Inside border	**¼ yd.**	**⅜ yd.**	**½ yd.**	**½ yd.**	**½ yd.**
1½" strips	**5**	**7**	**9**	**9**	**9**
Outside border	¾ yd.	1 yd.	1¼ yds.	1¼ yds.	1½ yds.
4½" strips	5	7	9	9	
5½" strips*					9
*Queen size only					

PIECING

Block 1

The background fabric is cut from the full width, so the strips must be cut in half to make the 22 sets.

1. Construct sets of strips according to the diagram below. The dark value represents scraps, and the light value is the common background fabric.

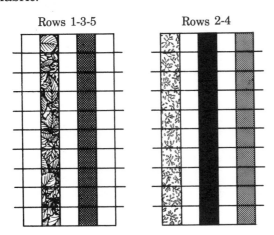

Rows 1-3-5   Rows 2-4

	Rows 1-3-5	Rows 2-4
Crib	6	4
Lap	10	7
Twin	18	12
Double/Queen	23	15

2. Press all seams so that they are either toward or away from the background fabric. This will simplify sewing the rows together.
3. Cut across these sets of strips at 2" intervals.

	Rows 1-3-5	Rows 2-4
Crib	51	34
Lap	93	62
Twin	174	116
Double/Queen	213	142

4. Sew rows together in the order shown:

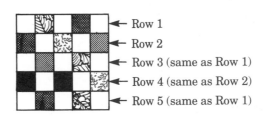

← Row 1
← Row 2
← Row 3 (same as Row 1)
← Row 4 (same as Row 2)
← Row 5 (same as Row 1)

Block 2

1. Using 5" wide strips of background and the remaining scrap strips, sew sets as follows:

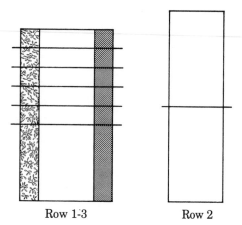

	Row 1-3	Row 2

Crib	4
Lap	7
Twin	12
Double/Queen	14

2. Cut Rows 1-3 sets at 2" intervals; cut rows as follows:

Crib	36
Lap	64
Twin	118
Double/Queen	144

3. For Row 2, cut 8" rectangles from the remaining 5" strips. You will need the following number of rectangles:

Crib	18
Lap	32
Twin	59
Double/Queen	72

4. Assemble Block 2 as shown:

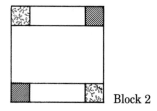

Block 2

5. Arrange the blocks, alternating Blocks 1 and 2. Block 2 is found in each corner of the quilt.

Crib	5 x 7
Lap	7 x 9
Twin	9 x 13
Double/Queen	11 x 13

6. Sew blocks together in rows; sew rows together, matching seams where required.

BORDERS

Borders on all but the queen size are optional. The quilt featuring this design on page 24 has two borders. The inside border is cut 1½" wide; the outside border is cut 4½" wide, except for the queen size, which is cut 5½" wide. Sew the strips together to achieve the length required. Measure borders as described on page 16, pin in place, and stitch.

Wild Goose Chase
Color photo on page 28

Color photo on page 28

**Double/
Queen
Size**

**Although Wild Goose Chase appears to be a
fairly complicated quilt to construct, it is de-
signed with just three different pieced units
set on the diagonal alternating with plain
squares. All the pieced blocks are made with
four half-square triangle units.**

Twin Size

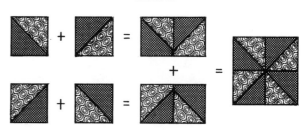

Wall Size

PIECING

1. There are three different arrangements of four half-square triangle units used in this quilt. The construction of the individual units is detailed below.

Unit 1

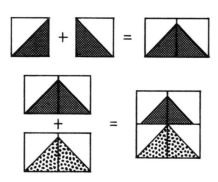

	Wall	Twin	Double/Queen
Blocks	16	96	168
Half-square triangle units	64	384	672

Construct each rectangle with two identical half-square triangle units; then, combine two different rectangles to make a Unit 1 block.

Unit 2

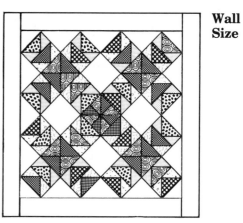

	Wall	Twin	Double/Queen
Blocks	1	15	30
Half-square triangle units	4	60	120

Make each of the Unit 2 blocks with four identical half-square triangle units.

Cutting Chart			
Block size (finished): 5"			
Quilt size	Wall	Twin	Double/Queen
without borders	28" x 28"	56" x 84"	84" x 98"
with borders	38" x 38"	66" x 94"	94" x 108"
Half-square triangle units			
Grid size (finished): 2½"			
Unit 1	**64**	**384**	**672**
Unit 2	**4**	**60**	**120**
Unit 3	**16**	**96**	**128**
Background	½ yd.	2 yds.	2¾ yds.
5½" squares	4	38	71
9½" squares for edge triangles	3	9	12
5½" squares for corner triangles	2	2	2
Inside border	**¼ yd.**	**⅜ yd.**	**½ yd.**
1½" strips	**4**	**7**	**9**
Outside border	⅝ yd.	1 yd.	1½ yds.
4½" strips	4	7	9

Unit 3

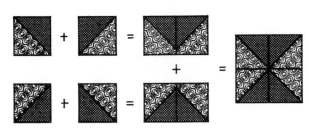

BORDERS

1. Join strips together to make pieces long enough for your borders.
2. Following directions for borders on page 16, measure, pin, and sew the narrow border first, then the wider one to the quilt top.

	Wall	Twin	Double/Queen
Blocks	4	24	42
Half-square triangle units	16	96	168

Make each of the Unit 3 blocks with four identical half-square triangle units.

2. For the edge triangles, cut the 9½" squares of background fabric diagonally into quarters.
3. For the corner triangles, cut the two 5½" squares of background fabric diagonally in half.
4. Arrange the units as shown in the diagram of the particular size quilt you are going to make (pages 51 and 52). Sew units together in rows; then, sew the rows together.

Good Fences Make Good Neighbors

Color photo on page 26

When I first saw this design in a photograph, it was done in Amish colors and looked difficult to make. Further analysis, however, showed it to be a simple block in a diagonal set. The name comes from the Robert Frost poem "Mending Wall" and refers to the scrap pinwheels kept separate by the "rail fence" strip between each group.

Cutting Chart

Block size (finished): 10"	
Quilt size	
without borders	70" x 84"
with borders	80" x 94"
Pinwheel blocks	50
Half-square triangle units	400
Grid size (finished): 2½"	
Fabric in 2 colors	1⅜ yds. each
3" x 10½" strips	50 each of 2 colors
Background fabric	1½ yds.
16½" squares for edge triangles	5
10½" squares for corner triangles	2
Border	1½ yds.
5½" strips	8

PIECING

1. Sew half-square triangle units together in sets of two.

2. Sew two sets of two together to form a pinwheel.

   Make 100 pinwheels.
3. Sew pinwheels together in sets of two.

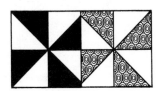

4. Sew one 3" x 10½" strip to each long side of the pinwheels, one color on each side. Make 50 blocks.

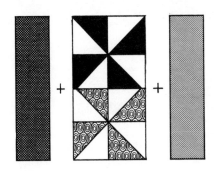

5. For edge triangles, cut squares in quarters diagonally. For corners, cut squares in half diagonally.
6. Arrange blocks according to the diagram on page 54. Keep the same fabrics going in a zig-zag line across the quilt. Add the edge and corner triangles.
7. Sew the blocks together in rows; sew the rows of the quilt together.

BORDERS

Add borders, if desired, following directions on page 16.

Split Ninepatch
Color photo on page 27

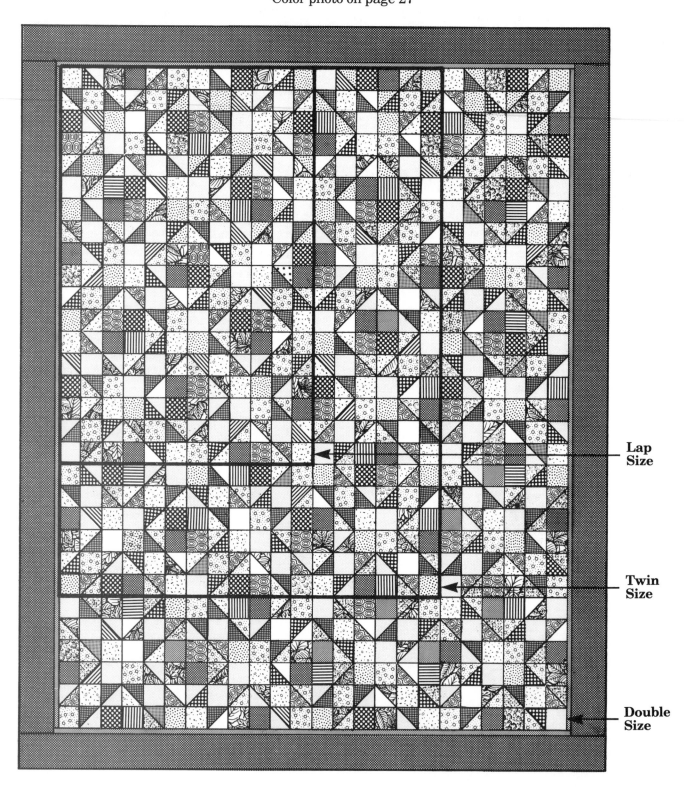

Lap Size

Twin Size

Double Size

While it may look difficult, the Split Nine-patch block is a simple one to make. When four of these blocks are put together and each is rotated one-quarter turn around the center, a starlike design is formed, with diagonal lines running through the whole quilt. Made with scraps, this quilt becomes a rich surface, with movement provided not only by the lines of the quilt but by the texture of the fabrics.

Cutting Chart			
Block size (finished): 9"			
Quilt size	Lap	Twin	Double
without borders	36" x 54"	54" x 72"	72" x 90"
with borders	46" x 64"	64" x 82"	82" x 100"
Split Ninepatch blocks	**24**	**48**	**80**
Half-square triangle			
units	96	192	320
Grid size (finished): 3"			
3½" squares			
Dark	48	96	160
Light	72	144	240
Inside border	¼ yd.	⅜ yd.	½ yd.
1½" strips	5	7	9
Outside border	**¾ yds.**	**1⅛ yds.**	**1¼ yds.**
4½" strips	5	8	9

PIECING

1. Following the diagrams below, piece the correct number of Split Ninepatch blocks for your quilt.

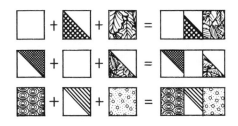

2. Join the blocks in groups of four as shown below.

3. Sew these larger blocks together in the following arrangement:

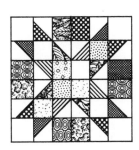

Lap	2 x 3
Twin	3 x 4
Double	4 x 5

BORDERS

1. Join strips together to make pieces long enough for your borders.
2. Following directions on page 16 for attaching borders, measure, pin, and sew the narrow border first, then the wider border, to the quilt top.

Confetti
Color photos on pages 29 and 30

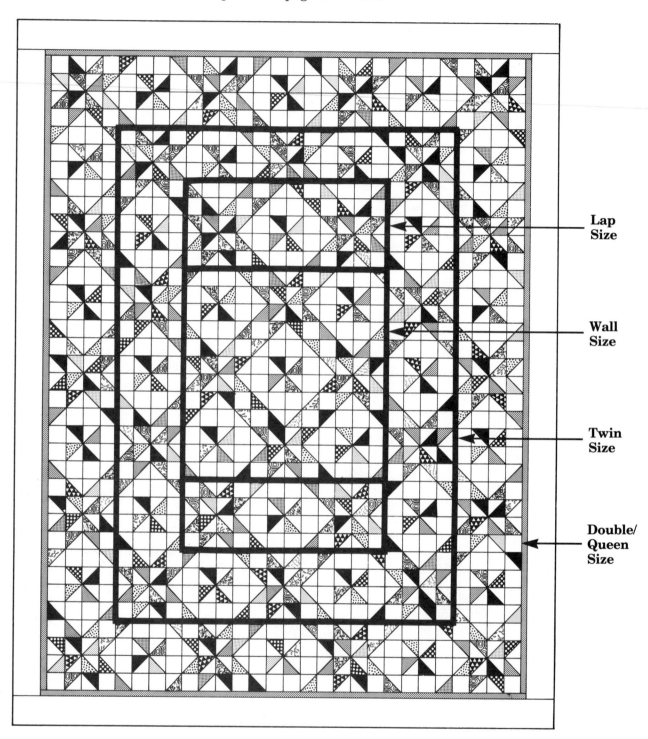

Lap
Size

Wall
Size

Twin
Size

Double/
Queen
Size

The combination of two fairly simple blocks, the Barbara Frietchie Star and an expanded Pinwheel block, yields a design that reminds me of confetti thrown at a parade. Dark and light combinations for the half-square triangle units and various light fabrics for the plain squares create the pattern.

Although the numbers of half-square triangle units may seem overwhelming, you can make 632 half-square triangle units from just 22 grids (see pages 10–11). If you cut plain squares from 3" strips, each strip will yield 14 squares, so you can cut 376 squares from just 27 strips.

Cutting Chart

Block size (finished):	10"			
Quilt size	Wall	Lap	Twin	Double/Queen
without borders	30" x 30"	30" x 50"	50" x 70"	70" x 90"
with borders	40" x 40"	40" x 60"	60" x 80"	80" x 100"
Pinwheel blocks	4	7	17	31
Star blocks	5	8	18	32
Half-square triangle units				
Grid size (finished): 2½"				
Dark/light	92	152	352	632
Background (light)	⅞ yd.	1 ⅜ yds.	2¾ yds.	5 yds.
3" squares	52	88	208	376
Inside border	¼ yd.	¼ yd.	⅜ yd.	½ yd.
1½" strips	4	5	7	9
Outside border	⅝ yd.	¾ yd.	1⅛ yds.	1¼ yds.
4½" strips	4	5	8	9

PIECING

Pinwheel Blocks

1. Each Pinwheel block and each Star block has one pinwheel. All the pinwheels can be made at the same time for a more organized approach. When the Pinwheel blocks are completed, set aside those needed for the Star blocks.

2. Sew pairs of half-square triangle units together as shown below, making sure that the position of the darks and lights remains consistent.

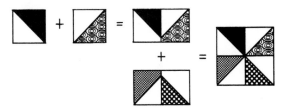

3. Matching the eight-point centers, sew pairs of these sets together, forming pinwheels.

4. To complete the Pinwheel blocks, sew pairs of squares together and sew one pair to opposite sides of each of the pinwheels required for the Pinwheel blocks.

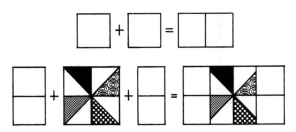

5. With the remaining pairs of squares, sew a half-square triangle unit to each end, making sure that the darks and lights are arranged in the proper order.

6. Sew these units to the top and bottom of the pinwheel units.

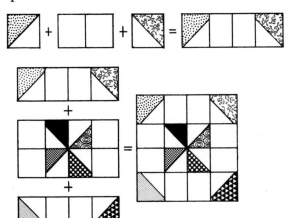

Star Blocks

1. Sew pairs of half-square triangle units together as shown. These will form the star points in your blocks.
2. Sew these to opposite sides of the reserved pinwheels.

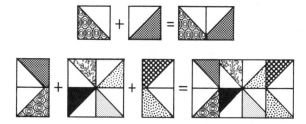

3. Sew a plain square to each end of the remaining triangle pairs; sew these units to the top and bottom of the pinwheel units.

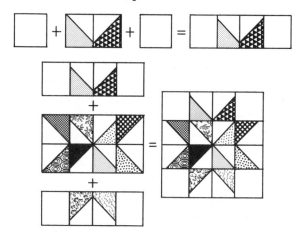

ASSEMBLY

1. Arrange the blocks, alternating a Star block with a Pinwheel block. Make sure that a Star block is in each corner of all but the wall-size quilt; a Pinwheel block is in each corner of the wall size.
2. Sew blocks together into rows; sew the rows together.

BORDERS

1. Join strips together to make pieces long enough for your borders.
2. Following directions on page 16 for attaching borders, measure, pin, and sew the narrow border first, then the wider border, to the quilt top.

Fireworks
Color photo on page 31

By varying the blocks in the Confetti design on page 58 rather than making each block the same, you can make a dynamic quilt that looks almost like a fireworks show on the Fourth of July. This quilt is a bit more complicated to make than most of the others in the book, but if you can follow a recipe and read a map, you will be able to complete it successfully. The block designs remain the same as for the Confetti quilt, but they are colored in several different ways, using different values for the backgrounds. Keeping the star points and pinwheel blades all the same color (but not necessarily the same fabric) and choosing bright colors for the corners and pinwheels of the Star blocks make

these design elements stand out. The following diagrams show you which values to put where and how many blocks of each type to make. The map shows just where each block belongs in the overall scheme. The value and color combinations of the half-square triangle units required are listed in the cutting chart on page 62.

If you use 3" finished half-square triangle units, the quilt will finish 60" x 84", and borders may be added, if desired. You can make it smaller by using 10" rather than 12" blocks. The smaller-size blocks will make the quilt 50" x 70" before adding borders. If you choose this option, make your finished grid size 2½" and cut the plain squares 3".

Cutting Chart		
Block size (finished)	10"	12"
Quilt size	Lap	Twin
without borders	50" x 70"	60" x 84"
Pinwheel blocks	7	17
Star blocks	8	18
Half-square triangle units		
Grid size (finished):	2½"	3"
Pinwheel color/dark	40	40
Pinwheel color/medium	24	24
Pinwheel color/light	4	4
Pinwheel corner/dark	40	40
Pinwheel corner/medium	24	24
Pinwheel corner/light	4	4
Star color/dark	88	88
Star color/medium	48	48
Star color/light	12	12
Star color/bright	72	72
Background squares	3"	3½"
Dark	80	80
Medium	48	48
Light	8	8
Bright	72	72

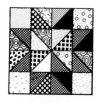

Block 4
Make 6

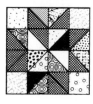

Block 5
Make 2

Block 6
Make 4

Block 7
Make 2

Block 8
Make 4

PIECING

1. The different blocks and the required numbers of each are shown below.

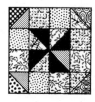

Block 1
Make 6

Block 2
Make 10

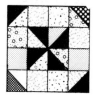

Block 3
Make 1

2. When all blocks are complete, arrange them according to the map below.

6	2	4	2	6
2	8	1	8	2
4	1	5	1	4
2	7	3	7	2
4	1	5	1	4
2	8	1	8	2
6	2	4	2	6

3. Sew the blocks together in rows; sew the rows together.

Although you do not see any borders on this quilt, they may be added, if desired (see page 16).

Ohio Star
Color photo on page 32

Double Size

While this quilt is traditionally made with just two or three colors, it also makes a wonderful scrap quilt. You can use the same fabrics for all the points of one star and make each star different from the next, or you can use different fabrics for each star point. The design is even more interesting when it is set on the diagonal. Different values of fabric also can be used for the alternating plain squares, giving the surface an added dimension and movement that enhances the overall appearance.

Before you begin this quilt, be sure to read the general directions for making quarter-square triangle units on page 11. The seam allowances used for constructing the quarter-square triangle units from half-square triangle units must be a consistent 1/4" in order for the measurements of the background squares to be accurate. Use a precise 1/4" measurement to sew these seams, rather than the edge of your presser foot. You may need to draw these seam allowances on your fabric.

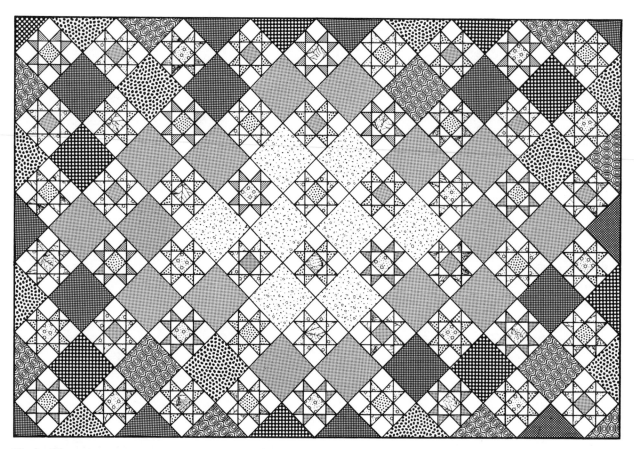

Twin Size

Lap Size

Cutting Chart

Block size (finished): 7⅞"			
Quilt size	Lap	Twin	Double
without borders	44" x 55"	66" x 99"	77" x 99"
Ohio Star blocks	20	54	72
Background blocks	12	40	56
Half-square triangle units	80	216	288
Grid size (finished): 3"			
Background squares			
3⅛" light	80	216	288
3⅛" medium	20	54	72
8⅜" light	2	6	20
8⅜" medium	4	16	10
8⅜" dark	6	16	24
14" squares for edge triangles	4	7	8
9" squares for corner triangles	2	2	2

PIECING

1. If you choose to make all the points of each star from the same fabric, you will need four matching half-square triangle units with a dark and light combination for each block. If all star points are different, choose any four half-square triangle units with a dark/light combination of fabrics for each block.
2. Following the general piecing directions on page 11, make quarter-square triangle units.
3. Using quarter-square triangle units and 3⅛" background squares, arrange and sew blocks together as shown below.

4. Cut the squares for the edge triangles diagonally in quarters to form triangles and cut the squares for the corner triangles diagonally in half. (See Diagonal Sets on pages 14–15.)
5. Using the Ohio Star blocks and the 8⅜" background squares and following one of the diagrams on page 63, arrange the blocks.
6. Sew the blocks together in rows; sew the rows together.

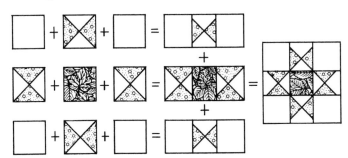

Cinderella

Color photo on page 25

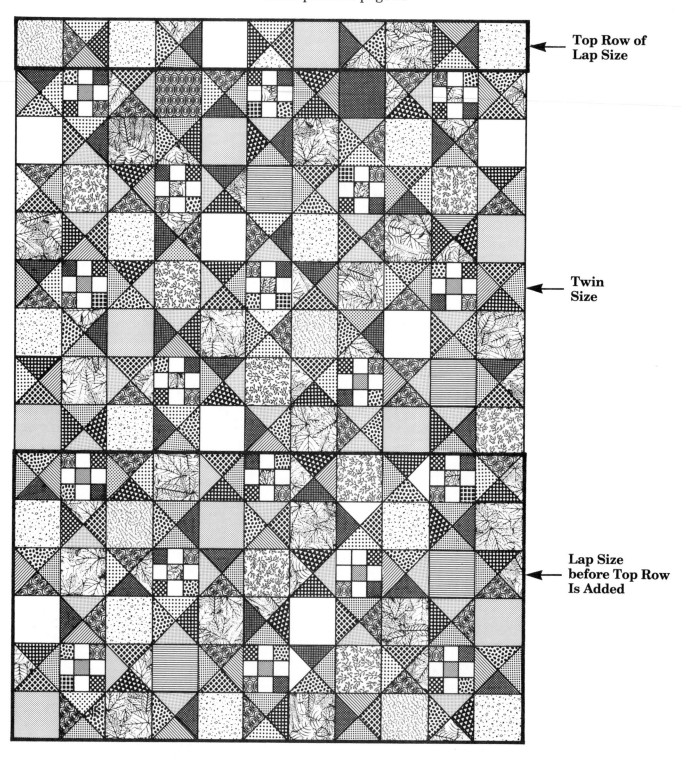

Top Row of
Lap Size

Twin
Size

Lap Size
before Top Row
Is Added

Like Cinderella, this quilt illustrates that
something lovely can come from very humble
beginnings. Also called Ninepatch Star, the
quilt is made from three simple units:
Ninepatches, quarter-square triangles, and
plain squares. Just two of them are pieced,
and the piecing is not difficult.

Cutting Chart		
Block size (finished): 6"		
Quilt size	Lap	Twin
without borders	42" x 66"	66" x 90"
Ninepatch units	**8**	**18**
2½" strips		
Light strips	6	13
Medium strips	6	14
Quarter-square triangle units		
Grid size (finished): 7¼"		
Two value	**3**	**5**
Three value	**8**	**18**
18" squares*		
Dark	5	16
Light	3	11
Medium	2	5
6½" background squares		
Medium	**7**	**17**
Light	**24**	**48**

*Reserved extra pieces for triangles (see Introduction, page 5)

PIECING

Ninepatch Units

1. Sew strips together in sets for Rows 1-3 . You will need two sets for the lap and five sets for the twin size.

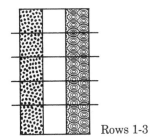

Rows 1-3

2. Sew strips together in sets for Row 2 of the Ninepatch unit. You will need two sets for the lap and four sets for the twin size.

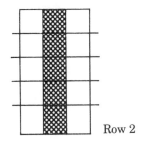

Row 2

3. Cut sets apart at 2½" intervals.
4. Assemble rows to make Ninepatch units.

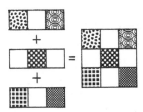

For the following steps, you must make a marking guide as described on pages 12–13 for a quarter-square triangle unit that finishes 6" square, or draw a grid of squares for quick-pieced triangles that is 7¼" square.

Quarter-Square Triangle Units (Two Value)

1. Placing dark and light fabrics right sides together, use your marking guide to draw squares on the wrong side of the lighter fabric.

2. Mark and sew as for Quick-Pieced Triangles (see pages 10–11).

3. Following the technique for quarter-square triangle units on page 11, place two half-square triangle units right sides together, match seams, and draw a line intersecting the seam line. Sew ¼" on either side of the line; cut apart on the drawn line.

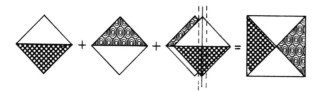

Quarter-Square Triangle Units (Three Value)

1. Draw grid squares using a combination of dark and light fabrics as described above. Mark and sew as for Quick-Pieced Triangles (see pages 10–11).

2. Using a combination of medium and dark fabrics, mark and sew the same number of squares as you did in step 1.

3. Press all seams toward the dark fabric.

4. Following the directions for quarter-square triangle units on page 11, place one dark/light square and one dark/medium square right sides together. Mark, stitch, and cut.

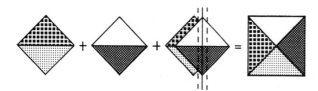

ASSEMBLY

1. Arrange all three units according to the diagram on page 66. The top row of the lap size is illustrated separately from the remainder of the quilt.

2. Sew units together in rows; sew rows together.

Quilt Finishing

There are many sources for information about basting and stitching quilts, either by hand or machine. Marsha McCloskey's *Lessons in Machine Piecing* or Trudie Hughes's *Template-Free™ Quiltmaking* have excellent directions for these techniques. I have not included them here because of their wide availability elsewhere.

Backings

Although some directions for quilt backings specify that seams should be lengthwise and away from the center of the quilt, I prefer to calculate the yardage required for the backs of my quilts to provide the least amount of excess. (Notice that I do not use the word "waste." All excess fabric from the back of my quilts becomes strips, half-square triangle units, or pieces for the front of other quilts. Nothing is wasted!)

For all quilts up to 84" long, I piece the backing with one crosswise seam in the center. To piece this backing, measure the width of the quilt, add 6", and double this measurement. This is the amount of fabric you will need to purchase in inches. (Divide by 36 to calculate yards.)

Back #1 up to 84" long

For quilts that are longer than 84" and up to 84" wide, I piece the backing with one lengthwise seam in the center. To piece this backing, measure the length of the quilt, add 6", and double this measurement. This is the amount of fabric you will need to purchase in inches.

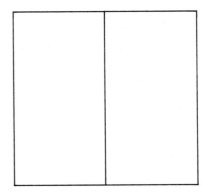

Back #2 up to 84" wide

Backings that need to be even larger than this are pieced with three lengths of fabric. To piece a backing of this size, measure the shortest side, add 6", triple this measurement, and purchase that amount of fabric in inches.

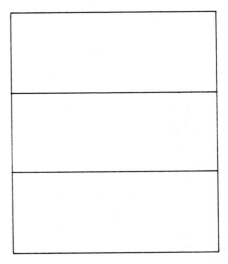

Back #3 up to 120" in either length or width

Bindings

General yardage amounts required for bindings can be found in the chart below:

Quilt Size	Yardage Requirements
Crib	$3/8$ yd.
Lap	$1/2$ yd.
Twin	$5/8$ yd.
Full/Queen	$3/4$ yd.

These measurements are very closely calculated and do not allow any extra fabric for mistakes in cutting. You may choose to purchase more than this, adding any extra yardage to your scraps.

Bindings for all my quilts are cut from the full width of the fabric in 2½" wide strips. To make the binding, sew the strips together to make one long strip. Press the strip in half, wrong sides together, pressing the seam allowances open. The strip should now be 1¼" wide. Open out the strip at one end and fold the corner to form a 45° angle. Refold the strip in half.

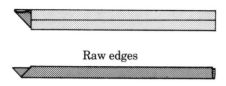

Raw edges

Do not trim the edge of the quilt after it has been quilted. Instead, wait until the binding has been sewn on. Beginning about 6" away from one corner, pin the binding strip to the edge of the quilt top, matching raw edges.   Pin to the next corner. To miter the corner, fold the binding strip at a 90° angle away from the quilt.

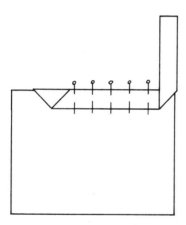

Fold the binding strip back on itself, parallel with the next edge of the quilt.

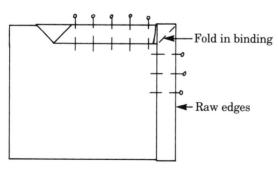

Fold in binding

Raw edges

Pin the miter; continue pinning the raw edges to the next corner. Repeat for each corner.

Where the end of the binding meets its beginning, open out the folded edge and place the end of the binding inside the fold. Refold the binding with the raw end inside.

Sew the binding with a ⅜" seam allowance. When you come to a corner, remove the pin at the miter, fold the miter toward you, and stitch to a point ⅜" from the end.

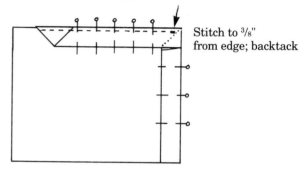

Stitch to ⅜" from edge; backtack

Cut the thread and remove the quilt from the sewing machine; refold the miter. Beginning at the raw edge, sew the next side of the quilt.

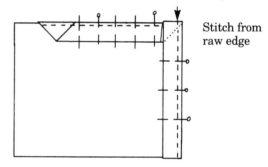

Stitch from raw edge

Repeat for each corner. Sew through all thicknesses where the two ends of the binding join.

Trim the edge of the quilt about ⅜" beyond the raw edge. Fold the binding over and hand stitch on the wrong side. At the corner, stitch the binding all the way to the edge of the quilt. Then, fold over the next edge; stitch. Be sure to stitch the entire corner closed.

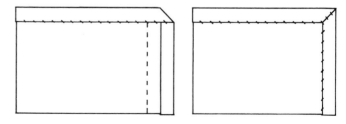

Hand stitch corner

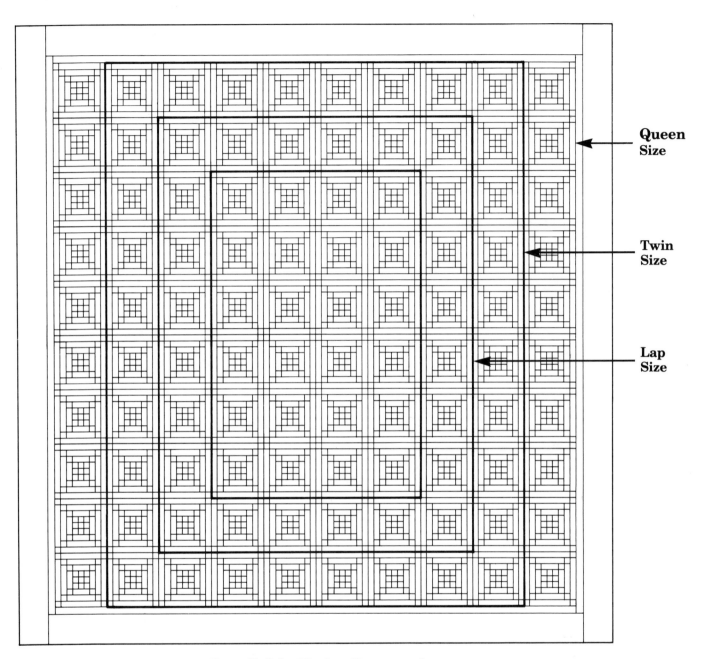

**Queen
Size**

**Twin
Size**

**Lap
Size**

Log Cabin Twice Removed
(pattern on page 40)

That Patchwork Place Publications and Products

BOOKS

Angelsong by Joan Vibert
Angle Antics by Mary Hickey
Appliqué Borders: An Added Grace by Jeana Kimball
Back to Square One by Nancy J. Martin
Baltimore Bouquets by Mimi Dietrich
A Banner Year by Nancy J. Martin
Basket Garden by Mary Hickey
Blockbuster Quilts by Margaret J. Miller
Calendar Quilts by Joan Hanson
Cathedral Window: A Fresh Look by Nancy J. Martin
Copy Art for Quilters by Nancy J. Martin
Corners in the Cabin by Paulette Peters
Country Threads by Connie Tesene and Mary Tendall
Even More by Trudie Hughes
Fantasy Flowers: Pieced Flowers for Quilters
     by Doreen Cronkite Burbank
Feathered Star Sampler by Marsha McCloskey
Fit To Be Tied by Judy Hopkins
Five- and Seven-Patch Blocks & Quilts for the ScrapSaver™
     by Judy Hopkins
Four-Patch Blocks & Quilts for the ScrapSaver
     by Judy Hopkins
Handmade Quilts by Mimi Dietrich
Happy Endings—Finishing the Edges of Your Quilt
     by Mimi Dietrich
Holiday Happenings by Christal Carter
Home for Christmas by Nancy J. Martin and Sharon Stanley
In The Beginning by Sharon Evans Yenter
Jacket Jazz by Judy Murrah
Lessons in Machine Piecing by Marsha McCloskey
Little By Little: Quilts in Miniature by Mary Hickey
Loving Stitches: A Guide to Fine Hand Quilting
     by Jeana Kimball
More Template-Free™ *Quiltmaking* by Trudie Hughes
My Mother's Quilts: Designs from the Thirties
     by Sara Nephew
Nifty Ninepatches by Carolann M. Palmer
Nine-Patch Blocks & Quilts for the ScrapSaver™
     by Judy Hopkins
Not Just Quilts by Jo Parrott
Ocean Waves by Marsha McCloskey and Nancy J. Martin
One-of-a-Kind Quilts by Judy Hopkins
On to Square Two by Marsha McCloskey
Osage County Quilt Factory by Virginia Robertson
Painless Borders by Sally Schneider
A Perfect Match: A Guide to Precise Machine Piecing
     by Donna Lynn Thomas

Picture Perfect Patchwork by Naomi Norman
Pineapple Passion by Nancy Smith and Lynda Milligan
A Pioneer Doll and Her Quilts by Mary Hickey
Pioneer Storybook Quilts by Mary Hickey
Quick & Easy Quiltmaking: 26 Projects Featuring Speedy
     Cutting and Piecing Methods by Mary Hickey,
         Nancy J. Martin, Marsha McCloskey & Sara Nephew
Quilts for All Seasons: Year-Round Log Cabin Designs
     by Christal Carter
Quilts from Nature by Joan Colvin
Quilts to Share by Janet Kime
Red and Green: An Appliqué Tradition by Jeana Kimball
Red Wagon Originals by Gerry Kimmel and Linda Brannock
Reflections of Baltimore by Jeana Kimball
Rotary Riot: 40 Fast and Fabulous Quilts by Judy Hopkins
     and Nancy J. Martin
Scrap Happy by Sally Schneider
Sensational Settings: Over 80 Ways to Arrange Your Quilt
     Blocks by Joan Hanson
Shortcuts: A Concise Guide to Metric Rotary Cutting
     by Donna Lynn Thomas
Shortcuts: A Concise Guide to Rotary Cutting
     by Donna Lynn Thomas
Small Talk by Donna Lynn Thomas
Smoothstitch™ *Quilts: Easy Machine Appliqué*
     by Roxi Eppler
Stars and Stepping Stones by Marsha McCloskey
Strips That Sizzle by Margaret J. Miller
Tea Party Time: Romantic Quilts and Tasty Tidbits
     by Nancy J. Martin
Template-Free™ *Quiltmaking* by Trudie Hughes
Template-Free™ *Quilts and Borders* by Trudie Hughes
Threads of Time by Nancy J. Martin
Women and Their Quilts by Nancyann Johanson Twelker

TOOLS

6" Bias Square®
8" Bias Square®
Metric Bias Square®
BiRangle™
Pineapple Rule
Rotary Mate™
Rotary Rule™
ScrapSaver™

VIDEO

Shortcuts to America's
Best-Loved Quilts

Many titles are available at your local quilt shop. For more information, send $2 for a color catalog to That Patchwork Place, Inc., PO Box 118, Bothell WA 98041-0118 USA.

☎ Call 1-800-426-3126 for the name and location of the quilt shop nearest you.